THE STONE BIRD

Books by Al Purdy

The Enchanted Echo, 1944
Pressed on Sand, 1955
Emu, Remember, 1956
The Crafte So Longe To Lerne, 1959
Poems for All the Annettes, 1962
The Blur in Between, 1963
The Cariboo Horses, 1965
North of Summer — Poems from Baffin Island, 1968
Poems for All the Annettes — Selected Poems Prior to 1965, 1968
The Quest for Ouzo, 1969
Love in a Burning Building, 1970
Selected Poems, 1972
Sex & Death, 1973
In Search of Owen Roblin, 1974
Hiroshima Poems, The Crossing Press, 1972
On the Bearpaw Sea, 1973
Sundance at Dusk, 1976
The Poems of Al Purdy, 1976
At Marsport Drugstore, 1977
No Other Country, 1977
A Handful of Earth, 1977
No Second Spring, 1978
Moths in the Iron Curtain, 1978
Being Alive, 1978

Books edited by Al Purdy

The New Romans — Candid Canadian Opinions of the U.S., 1968
Fifteen Winds, 1969
Storm Warning, 1971
Storm Warning 2, 1976

THE STONE BIRD

AL PURDY

McCLELLAND AND STEWART

Copyright © 1981 Al Purdy

All rights reserved

The Canadian Publishers
McClelland and Stewart
25 Hollinger Road
Toronto M4B 3G2

Canadian Cataloguing in Publication Data

Purdy, Alfred W., 1918-
　The stone bird

Poems.

ISBN 0-7710-7212-0 pa.

I. Title.

PS8531.U73S86　C811'.54　C80-094845-9
PR9199.3.P87S86

Printed and bound in Canada by
T. H. Best Printing Company Limited

For Eurithe and for Dennis Lee

"... the irresistible anxiety to discover what the orange whistles and the invisible globes on the other side of death were like."

Gabriel Garcia Marquez

CONTENTS

Part One

The Dead Poet / *13*
Journey to the Sea / *15*
Bestiary / *17*
South of Durango / *20*
Figures of Earth / *22*
D.H. Lawrence at Lake Chapala / *25*
Near Patzcuaro / *27*
At Paricutin Volcano / *29*
In the Garden / *31*
Beyond the Mountains of Heaven / *33*
Birdwatching at the Equator / *35*
Moses at Darwin Station / *37*
Darwin's Theology? / *41*
Moonspell / *42*
Driving the Spanish Coast / *44*
Meeting / *47*
On the Hellas Express / *50*
Instant at Pompeii / *51*
Small Wars / *53*

Part Two

Shot Glass Made From a Bull's Horn / *57*
Near Tofino, Vancouver Island / *58*
The Nurselog / *60*
Hail Mary in Dawson City / *62*
Across the Mary River. . . / *64*
Red Fox on Highway 500 / *66*
May 23, 1980 / *69*
In the Snow / *71*
Spinning / *73*
Inside Gus / *74*
Night Softball / *75*
No Second Spring / *76*
Mantis / *82*

The Darkness / *83*
Fathers / *85*
Norma's Poem / *86*
Found Among the Effects / *87*
For Bumper — who can't read / *89*
Who Killed D'Arcy McGee? / *91*
Angus Unlimited / *95*
Cosmos / *97*
Seasons / *98*
Goodbye / *100*
Writer-in-Rez / *102*
The Stone Bird / *105*

Acknowledgements / *109*

PART ONE

THE DEAD POET

I was altered in the placenta
by the dead brother before me
who built a place in the womb
knowing I was coming:
he wrote words on the walls of flesh
painting a woman inside a woman
whispering a faint lullaby
that sings in my blind heart still

The others were lumberjacks
backwoods wrestlers and farmers
their women were meek and mild
nothing of them survives
but an image inside an image
of a cookstove and the kettle boiling
— how else explain myself to myself
where does the song come from?

Now on my wanderings:
at the Alhambra's lyric dazzle
where the Moors built stone poems
a wan white face peering out
— and the shadow in Plato's cave
remembers the small dead one
— at Samarcand in pale blue light
the words came slowly from him
— I recall the music of blood
on the Street of the Silversmiths

Sleep softly spirit of earth
as the days and nights join hands
when everything becomes one thing
wait softly brother
but do not expect it to happen
that great whoop announcing resurrection
expect only a small whisper
of birds nesting and green things growing
and a brief saying of them
and know where the words came from

JOURNEY TO THE SEA

Zig-zag on the switchback road
over mountain country
in alpine clarity
trees have eaten their shadows
and many-fingered cactus
stand like prophets
pointing in all directions
to the Promised Land
Then down to the tropics
in sweatbox heat
and comet-blossoms of flowers
the yellow torch of primavera
a blue one for jacaranda
tents of blue-yellow
as the man-beetle floats down
— floats heavily down
with a pig-squeal of tires
Then a road not on maps
still being built
by prehistoric engineers
I daydream in the heat
of seeing a man waving
a red flag on the road
shouting Turn Back Turn Back
We slosh and dribble
thru thin brown rivers
near half-built bridges
and overturned wheelbarrows
— a crashed airplane at roadside
mashed aluminum bug
the pilot certainly dead
and thinking: how awful to die
reeling down from up there
allotting yourself just seconds
to remember the best things

counting from one to twenty
— eight my love and six my love
and three for yellow primavera
and then forgetting
Washouts and stone slides
where the mountain spared us
by acting a moment before
we came or a moment after
At the world's last corner
a mountain shelf
maybe a thousand feet high
and nothing but space
an empty blue room
— and if there was anywhere
a First Cause
it had hidden itself perfectly
by remaining in plain sight
without intention or design
blue robes and blue sandals
spread out before us
like the altar cloths of heaven
an aching majesty of nothing
while we drink beer

                    Mexico

BESTIARY

Burro sounds
in early morning
six eight ten syllables of a rusty iron gate
squeaking open and closed
the long guttural word of speaking
that hears itself from outside the burro's body
earth-wail of the burro-soul
and hairy old man's ears lift listening
unheavenly jew'sharpgutstretchingmouthfartingmusic
stymies sleep
touching the far rim of being
the solemn lost edge of things
when the first cry was a new thing
that said this is who I am
and to hell with mountains

Mourning doves
roosting in eucalyptus trees
above flaming poinsettia
a throaty non-bird sound
gurgling insomniac sound
that goes whispering back and twists
itself into serpent hiss
old father of lies on his crawling belly
reptilian ancestor without song
goes slumbering back to the great lizards
kin to the lizard
chickadee chirp
in a snake's mouth

Rooster boast
two short and one long syllable
sends blood plummeting skyward
where he can no longer go
and declares in rooster
earth is best earth is best
and heart knows that isn't true
the brag-song is a grief-cry
earth at best is second-best
he mourns the sky the lost sky
with a metal windvane rooster
dodging lightning atop a northern barn
he is sky-lost
the white stovelid a lost glory
poor flightless bird

Dogs
barking and threatening
harassing each other
then into the mob-gabble and out
again emerges one long wavering howl
so close to the man-howl in extremis
self-pitying man-cry
all is lost all is lost
then moving along the scale down down
the dog-soul plaintive and wavering
saying piteously
I am so lonely so one-single

I have so much personality
such tragic grandeur
then frightening himself into seriousness
a disembodied ghost-voice trembling
among red pomegranate and mango trees
calling Father Dog and Grandfather Wolf
all the way back to the Cambrian
and Precambrian when there were no wolves
no housepets
only the still cooling world
earth steaming and boiling
in the ovens of creation

                      Mexico

SOUTH OF DURANGO

It begins: a forest of men
not whatever man is
but non-human beings
green men standing on tiptoe
cactus you might say
and be neither wrong nor right
— the sun stops thundering
there in silence exactly like noise
a lake of silence and the green men
waiting there waiting waiting
century after century after century
the same at either end
You stop the radiator bubbles
road completely empty
nearby a miniature green dragon
iguana among the green men
this is not the story I am from
a fraction left or right of reality
— somewhere a woman
is screen-tested to play
Scarlett O'Hara in her dreams
and smiles unerringly at the bedpost
here an enormous snake
fills the entire dry creek bed
instead of water
and the radiator bubbles
— hallucinatory
the Ford growls Detroit
turn up the radio
on to Zacatecas
noise exactly like silence
in which you think

"How far to Zacatecas?"
a dead burro near the road
and some vultures eating it
in which you think
of Graham Greene and Evelyn Waugh
who hated Mexico
for scenes like this and others
but not indifference hate nor love
are valid in this country
only the green men standing forever
are valid without complexity
I drink a beer driving
with one hand while our shadow
a phantom Detroit
races on ahead with a feeling
as if someone had driven
a motor car into my soul
and yesterday is fast arriving
bringing Voltaire and Mme. du Chatelet
equipped with measuring devices
to determine whether I have one

                                      Mexico

FIGURES OF EARTH

Kept dogs are all flesh
but wild dogs are partly spirit
and sing in the kept dogs' sleep
how to kill your masters
Burros say A-haw A-haw
     or sometimes a-Haw a-Haw
and they know the difference
tethered to all the billions
of tons of the earth's body
they believe the world
is tethered to them
when they refuse to move
the world is make-believe
Horses stand in the sun
sometimes with a halo of flies
(once in a dry field of thistles
I saw the new shape
of a dead burro becoming
and he was moving
farther and farther away
from what he had been
with an escort of flies)
Here the snakes
are only accidentally visible
when you tie a shoelace
and it squirms
lizards squirrels brown birds
so common you multiply by ten
to know they are there
In all these creatures' minds
there is a god
when they sleep
they see God in their dreams
a mountain lion

who kills them asleep
but awake they are alive
God is a bronze god
but they are colour-blind
so he is a grey shadow
under the dead grey moon
he provides no salvation
no loaves nor fishes
he is hungry
they are food
God dreams of food
and his wander-creatures
under the organ cactus
in parched arroyos
like cupboard drawers
of the desert
are a sacrifice:
their screams are praise
their cries are hymns of praise
He sleeps on the mile-high
Mexican plateau
a yellow god
in the shape of God
and dreams of food
and food is everywhere
God hears food
A-haw a-Haw
or sub-sonic whispers
of manna register
in his eating dream
God dreams:
he is half inside the dream
and half out
he cannot move
all that food
shouts in his waking brain
but his legs are still asleep

A-haw a-Haw like mockery
but God is not mocked
for long and soon
in the dry cold dark
a feather of light
and then the pink tongue
of mountain dawn

                Mexico

D.H. LAWRENCE AT LAKE CHAPALA

Try to simplify your life
you cannot
try to live a new life
and the old one complicates the new
— today's details like sand grains like commas
mind-lost in an immense
garbage heap of yesterday's details
yet I am preoccupied by this phoenix
with moulting tail-feathers:
Lawrence grows small in the midst of all this
— this lost importance this scribble of things
How could you pick him out now
see him from one corner of your eye
scrubbing the tile floor at Zaragoza 4
throbbing with tubercular life
bossing Frieda around on Chapala beaches
and why for gawd's sake do you want to?
answer: for your own sake only

A fly speck seen from fifty miles up
memory dismisses him
he's dead long after his death
fading despite all those once-shining thoughts
disagreeable little prick
a bit anti-Semitic and self-important
— get the hell outa my head
begone take off split get lost et cetera
and finally incredibly I find myself
arguing with him saying:
"Lissen you one-fifth Cockney bastard
(I'm anti-Cockney) you're a liar
life is marvellous only
when you're in love
with a woman-echo or your own genius
Murry had you pegged but good
too bad it was him tho he being
only 'one-fifth of a mud-coloured man'

Whaddaya say to that Lawrence whaddaya say?"
Apotheosis takes over
and he says he's like "some horrid hairy God
the Father in a William Blake imagination"
That kinda stops me that really stops me and
he all the time coughing his guts out
where nobodaddy listens to plasma-gargle
soaking the drainpipes of God

His vehemence fades not at all
among the details random details
that litter the brain's red dung-heap
cover the real earth and mind-place
we hold that is private ourselves
resist knowing we're only details
demand glory require importance
somebody cut the sky's throat when we die
strike up the band rouse the horsemen of God
And Lawrence
no doubt he wanted that too
illusion the endless infusion he lived by
so real when Frieda remembered long after
and tried to repeat them the song
of the senses hymns of the dark gods
she could only stutter the details
to some young interviewer some boy
with steno pad and the best of intentions
stutter the details of Lawrence
and they sounded so mundane and meaningless
sounded so flat and commonplace
the kid gave up Great Literature
and opted for forensic medicine instead
Of course they are flat and commonplace
but not meaningless
— not when you remember the details of Lawrence
and include the glowing question mark he wrote
after every single one
of the million names of God?

       Mexico

NEAR PATZCUARO

Sun dominates
a glass ball dashing back and forth
in the space between your eyes
It's like a disease you catch
but after exposure to fire-germs
a cure is effected
when the bugs begin to love you
Arriving from the 16th century
dugout canoes with fishermen
and the death-mask of Father Morelos
inside his 132-foot statue
gleams across Lake Patzcuaro
blessing damn near everything
which includes Indians market women
and near the *farmacia* a dog
with arched back shitting
I have to learn how it is
to be alive here all over again
do as the brown people do
and their don'ts a dance step
I look out from a blind beggar's eyes
and see myself a northern myth
a tall grey gringo illness
and shudder away from me
Driving to Tzintzuntzan
Place of the Hummingbirds
ancient Tarascan capital
I learn how they defeated the Aztecs
in battle by shouting
Tzin-tzun-tzan at them
reducing Tenochtitlan to a whisper
of many hummingbirds' wings

How to be alive again?
Did Father Morelos know
or Bishop Don Vasco de Quiroga
with their transplanted God?

— the flowers with their brilliant
rainbow faces turn
toward the mountain morning
— among the innocent mountains
unnoticed are the guilty ones
where 500 dormant volcanoes shudder
whatever uncertainties there are
expressed in that shudder
— and love which is the inexpressible
turn to me in this place
and from my continual turmoil
grant me some knowledge of myself
and of my residence on earth

                              Mexico

AT PARICUTIN VOLCANO*

Si Señor — devil there
he live cornfield
he spit black smoke
he spit white smoke
he spit fire
Devil grow grow
he lil black chicken
he big my house
he mountain black mountain
spit black dirt
spit black dirt my village
I call priest
he come say holy words
he say devil in earth
devil want come out
he say holy words stop devil
no stop devil
devil too strong
keep on coming
We run — Maria run
— Jesus run — Consuela run
— all run
devil keep on coming
Jesus Maria Consuela dead
no corn grow
Hear bell ring now
church bell under stone?
— devil ring church bell
he want us think he priest
he want us come there
pray him
we no come

Devil under earth
ring church bell
call come home
we no live there
he say we his children
we no his children
we no come
Por favor Señor — pesos?

                    Mexico

*Paricutin volcano sprouted out of a cornfield overnight, in Michoacan State near Acuapan, February 20, 1943. One day it wasn't there; on the following morning the infant volcano was a hundred feet tall, with smoke and rock pouring into the sky from its mouth. A week later *"El Monstruo"* had grown to 550 feet, overwhelming two Tarascan Indian villages with lava and ash. The yellow church steeple of one buried village is still visible; the other settlement has completely disappeared, church and all.

IN THE GARDEN

Poinsettias blaze red bougainvillaea burn
the lake is a smooth blue plate
for sun-tongues to lick clean
Once maybe at the very beginning of things
everything was mud-coloured
you could look out and see only grey sand
you could see nothing to send messages
back from it to you
just dirty-coloured seawater
where rain had lashed things in fury
and wind mixed everything up like soft porridge
and only the pole star shone like a white lever
for gods of the sky to shinny down
on long slender columns of light
and arrive on earth with a cry
Then we had blue and scarlet and silver
then we had vegetable love
whoever was looking for something
dreamed it first of all
then we made a wanting song of sadness
then we made a finding song of joy
when the Moon said "Here I am Sun"
so he was
and went on sailing up there
all night for the first time

It must have been if you were watching
if you could have watched in the morning
a time to stand naked in rain
a time to feel the fingers of warm rain
touching your new human body
and stammer some praise for it
        your thanks — and you had to thank someone

why not the earth?
Thank you earth thank you sea thank you sky
the beginnings of human love
when we said:
        these things are dear
they are bought with your life
they are yours for only an instant
they are yours unconditionally
then you must give them away

                          Mexico

BEYOND THE MOUNTAINS OF HEAVEN

In the blue city of Timur
an old man outside a mosque
obviously praying with open eyes
a very old man who did not care
about the tourists and young soldiers
from Moscow passing and watching him
curiously like some mindless freak
in Asia a long way from Red Square
and the drum-roll of marching armies
I think he didn't even notice
or realize they were looking at him
he just kept praying — and I noted
deep lines around his mouth
nose big like a hill on his face
eyes talking to his own far gods
that archaeologists dig up sometimes
in the form of baked clay
and transport west of the Caucasus
— under the traditional Uzbek hat
black with silver trimming
talking to gods I don't know
but vaguely surmise in his mind
(and swirling around us
ghost horsemen on desert ponies
drinking goat's milk and mare's blood
in felt tents lost in yellow distance)
gods like nerve endings
I don't know them
but pray along with him anyway
for what's important
and has nothing to do with armies
inferring the complex and difficult
but finally this simplicity

that blots out the blue mosque
as Samarcand denies Ameliasburg
and knows what it knows:
silence in him this long silence
near the noisy Sunday market
with green melons and shishkebob
and charcoal burners smoking
an old man with a big nose
deep lines around his mouth
having joined himself here
and permitted this intrusion

    Samarcand, Uzbekistan

BIRDWATCHING AT THE EQUATOR

The blue-footed booby
stands on her tropic island
in the Galapagos group
stands all day long
shading her eggs from the sun
also protecting her blue feet
from too much ultraviolet
Sometimes the male booby
flaps his wings and dances
to entertain his mate
pointing his toes upward
so they can discuss blueness
which seems to them very beautiful
Their only real enemy
is the piratical frigate bird
floating on great black wings
above the mile-long island
Sometimes the frigate bird
robs them of their fish
whereupon the booby
is wont to say "Friggit"
and catches some more
When night comes all the boobies
sit down at once as if
God had given them a signal
or else one booby says
to the rest "Let's flop boys"
and they do

The blue booby's own capsule-
comment about evolution:
if God won't do it for you
do it yourself:
stand up
sit down
make love
have some babies
catch fish
dance sometimes
admire your feet
friggit:
what else is there?

        Galapagos Islands

MOSES AT DARWIN STATION

Tortoises
like small boxcars
a baker's dozen of them
one seven hundred pounds
and 160 years old
(call him Moses
pre-dating Darwin's
Voyage of the Beagle)
body a huge strongbox
plundered by 18th-
century seamen for food
but nearly impregnable
for non-human burglars
We're shadows to him
two-legged shadows
ungainly whirlpools
of bifurcated motion
black and white only
in his optic register
the scrawny old-man's neck
motionless buckboard of shell
galumphing *galapago*
exploring silence
investigating the either/
or of persistent rumours
that God exists
or does not
Scratch his long neck
and he suffers me
after 160 years
one can afford
indulgence of shadows
tolerance of transience

Tortoise-*chelonia*
science nomenclature
animal identity
and yet I think
who are they?
despite trite labels
perishable description
vanishing sound-glyphs
who are they?
— would I recognize Moses
in a downtown galaxy
or asteroid hotel room
of neon and strippers
in New York and Vegas
his buckboard shell
traversing 160 years
his ponderous ancestors
hop-stepping ages
reptilian acrobat
one hundred million years
of fence posts of time
a phantom charioteer
called soul or spirit
or even instinct
urging him on forever
We of course are human
but not recognizably so
as long as he was tortoise
in fact confess it:
remembering far ages
when birds and mammals
branched off from reptiles
and therefore those distant
ancestors of old Moses
are unrecognizably
but yet indubitably
my own

It is chastening
it is downright chastening
to have your forefather
barely acknowledge you
when you scratch his neck
but snuff at greenstuff
you proffer cautiously
his pleasantly ugly
face a road map
to your own past

Therefore go back there
following your footprints
a lost time-traveller
when things were beginning:
while comets crash
and ricochet on earth
the *phyla*-families
take evasive action:
one-celled *protozoa*
dodges fire-balls
way back in the Cambrian
worm-*annelid* slips the punch
fish-*chordata* becomes
a clumsy amphibian
and seven-come-eleven
the dice turn snake eyes
tortoise-*chelonia*
does a tricky dance step
and we're on our way
Ol Granpappy Moses
brushes off this nonsense
of uranium clocks
and scientific theories
of continental drifting
glaciation and star-birth
remembering only

the linchpin now
this permanent moment
the same as always
its name is Moses

    Galapagos Islands

Note: *Galapago* is a Spanish word for tortoise, *chelonia* the zoological one for tortoise. *Phyla* is another zoological term, embracing more than twenty species of early animal life, each of which was responsible for many succeeding variations of itself. The Cambrian period in geology is that time when life began on earth, some 500 million years ago.

DARWIN'S THEOLOGY?

— stand under the great sky round
            circling these islands
where the absence of a god
leaves a larger vacuum
than a presence could fill
with a presence
sea and sky completely occupied
by the non-existent monster

                    Galapagos Islands

MOONSPELL

I have forgotten English
in order to talk to pelicans
plunging into tomorrow
disturb the deep reverie
of herons standing
on yesterday's shoreline
find the iguana's secret
name embroidered
on his ruby brain
It is milk
it is moonlight
milk pouring
over the islands
stand in a doorway
listen
I am drowning
in sky milk
and those soft murmurings
of moonlit vertebrae
these deciphered codewords
are spoken names
of island dwellers
they will not be repeated
pour on my bare shoulders
are small extensions
of themselves
as the manta ray bubbles
rising in water
gleams in moonlight
small fish tremble
I know I know
my speech is grunts
squeaks clicks stammers
let go let go

follow the sunken ships
and deep sea creatures
follow the *protozoa*
into that far darkness
another kind of light
leave off this flesh
this voice these bones
sink down

    Galapagos Islands

DRIVING THE SPANISH COAST

Other men's thoughts haunting me
on this Mediterranean coast:
Robert Browning sailing past Cadiz Bay
into which sunset ran reeking
in order to make a poem
(Home Thoughts from Abroad)
And these ruined stone watchtowers
from which thoughts were flung
via flashing mirror and burning torch
relayed from tower to tower:
"Phoenicians are coming"
"Roman galleys on the horizon"
"Greek triremes nearing the coast"
— and their gods like specks of popcorn
hovering anxiously in the high blue
awaiting the battle's outcome
on which their existence depended
And Drake at Cadiz
"singeing King Philip's beard"
the smell of burned hair absent
now only garbage and gasoline
on a road near Algeciras
with sandwiches and beer
Supplanting other impressions
paleolithic caves at Nerja
and 20,000-year-old cave paintings
which Browning didn't see
and Drake wouldn't have noticed
where some two-legged animal
able to think abstractly
and so create in his mind
the running deer and mammoth
decided that written symbols
were strong magic
and travel by mathematics

to string clichés 200,000 miles
across the planet's moon
— long ago
I reached that place
in childhood when I was a far traveller
touched down at Mare Imbrium
and the Sea of Serenity
but left no trace
Anyway
in these conjectures
Browning would have had a different poem
if Nerja had been known in his time
and Drake sail backward to the paleolithic
instead of circumnavigating the globe?
Myself musing
how the earth itself is all things
its shapes greater than imagination
preconceiving all our discoveries
all artifacts of man duplicated
in caves and desert places
given grace here and non-utility
given silence that is not our silence
earth having invented these chattering apes
is responsible and may not dispense with them
grants them tenure of their lives
certain moments degrees of understanding
and to whom we might in all respect
address these shapes of wisdom
"Our Father which art the earth!"
— this short silence
I have initiated
this brief dash after
the exclamation mark
is about to join itself to eternity
Now yesterday's signal towers:
on which I project the personal-abstract
the time-travelling verb
the space-eating lexicon

of rocket sounds
relayed from tower to tower
— seeing myself
an ageing man driving a small car
half an inch longer than his knees
seeing himself from a long way off
balanced ten miles up in the sky
like a speck of popcorn
observing the coloured tin can moving
a blink of blue at the sea's edge
a man-shape flickering and inconstant
among Greeks Romans and Phoenicians
in an exercise of double vision
myself an unemployed shaman
painting star visitors
with vegetable dyes and blood
red ochre in the caves at Nerja
— then nothing

                Spain

MEETING

The cave entrance was small
he had to scrunch over while entering
which made it difficult to hold onto
the pine torch in one hand and stone spear
in the other and still see where he was going
But the cave widened and opened
into a series of vaulted stone rooms
each with an eerie echo of his own footsteps
His eyes darted fearfully
as far into darkness
as the hissing torch would explore
and to frighten off spirits
he waved the spear in a threatening motion
and eyes gleamed back at him
It might be only the eyes of a cave bear
and that was bad enough
but if the torch should die
spirits of mammoth wolves aurochs
and the spirit of One-Eye
the tribe's dead witch-doctor
who had hated him
— these could swarm from the darkness
and surround his own spirit
and tear his name from his mouth
so that he could give no answer
to the babbling voices

He howled and howled
in a frenzy of fear
like the People's dogs
when the moon takes them
He ran toward the cave entrance
and darkness fled on ahead of him
but his sense of direction had failed
the pale light which had seemed safety
turned into an immense shape of glowing stone
that pulsated and throbbed inside itself

The earth possessed a womb
old as earth is old
cream-coloured smooth stone
hidden in blood darkness
with a surrounding network
of creamy ganglions and nerves
in which light flickered and danced
leading away from the glowing centre
to join the body of earth
— something awakened inside the man
as if he had just been born
and looked at the new world
outside himself
with a vast surprise
— he listened to a voice
inside that did not speak
wetness sang between his legs
blood churned and accelerated
so that he seemed to himself
to be running and running
but the stone had not moved
— whatever this magic was
he had touched its centre
something brooding
solemn as very early morning
when nothing moves or speaks or growls
with light glowing in all things
— it flowed thru him
he swayed
as trees sway in a moving wind
or grass dances in lilting summer
his head left his body
and knees weakened
he fell down

The man's name was Man
Man turned away with his added strength
which some would think weakness
with his knowledge that could be ignorance
his body turning and returning
in the direction from which he had come
with dying torch in his left hand
he felt movement on his right
a little stir of wind of passage
perhaps only a bat perhaps
a man from another time
or even the dead One-Eye
Man went away to find Woman
and say this thing to her
knowing he would return later
moving toward the cave entrance
that changed from soft vagueness
to a patch of summer sky
— and the Stone knew

                The Caves of Nerja
                Costa del Sol, Spain

ON THE HELLAS EXPRESS

We were two and claimed it
but the compartment could hold six
      — sometimes we saw the other four
      looking in our window
      from the outside corridor
      with tired faces
      and pulled the curtain
      hurriedly
All the way from Luxembourg
thru Germany Austria and Yugoslavia
to Greece we guarded that compartment
slept in shifts
left singly to bring back food
crept out at night for air
thru snowy mountain villages
and dark night streets of towns
in Alexander's Macedonia we galumphed
triumphant North Americans
street lights lamp lights starlight
shining on our grey blankets sideways
Of course an officious little official
helped us at the barricades
thinking we might be important
and wanted a good word placed
in a superior ear in Athens
And we chuckled
pleased to be so clever
      — drank tea in Austria
      beer in Germany
      ate our sandwiches
      in Yugoslavia
where Tito's brand of socialism flourished
while those four other people
waited outside
And years later
we are still defending that compartment

INSTANT AT POMPEII

Modestus drinking wine
sits in the brothel
listening to his millstones
grind wheat next door
slaves turning them
and says to friend Rufus
"Maceas is like a bull
he never tires. . . . "
Women buy bread outside
money falls on stone
Beyond the city wall
Vesuvius broods
Rufus: "More wine"
On the Via del Lupanare
carriages rattle
and market wagons
in the hot summer morning
sparks from iron wheels
sting the legs of passersby
and they shrink back
from lunging horses
Livia of the freckled breasts
brings wine
tossing her head
at remarks about her
and flies buzz in one corner
Down the street
a scribe works swiftly
composing a letter
to an old woman's son
saying "Come home soon
that red wine you like
waits beside your bed
in case the shops are closed
Do you remember Livia?
— she asks about you

The work is long
but I will see you
in the early morning
before I have to go
if you're not asleep then —"

SMALL WARS

       — there are wars
like fingernails versus toenails
like blood in a fresh woodland stream
where bodies float down to the ocean
                bumping over stones

       there are wars sometimes
in birch woods and pine forests
brother against brother on sunlit mornings
and looking into the eyes of the living one
             see the dead brother

       there are battles
in which the dead men look so peaceful
and the living so maimed by death
you would think they were the corpses
             and found their way home

       on Armistice Day
old men marching in the rain
water shining on horn-rimmed glasses
and the bugle sounds Taps like a weeping woman
for old men who survived and young men who didn't
but November rain can't be anything but November rain
             with wet poppies and noses running

PART TWO

SHOT GLASS MADE FROM A BULL'S HORN
    — once owned by Ralph Purdy

A young ensign set lips to this cup.
I drink from it now. In 1815,
one Francis Gore, Lieutenant Gov.
of Upper Can., gave him his commish.
The cup is dark brown with gold lights.
It's attractive to me for such reasons,
with initials R.P. deeply incised,
and a crude Brit. flag cut in bone.
I presume R.P. was my ancestor,
when George something-or-other was king,
at a time when the French Rev. was
alarming grocers: Ralph went swaggering
into a pub full of joy in himself,
and talked nonsense in some girl's ear:
after the fiasco of 1812,
love was the thing and war a bore.
Here's to you Ralph with good rye,
when kings are quaint and Canada is
a country ending at the beginning,
but love and sex continue thru history:
somewhere a phantom ensign is waving his sword,
and somewhere his backwoods Jerusalem survives:
wholly ridiculous and quite unreal,
where the great trees stand and a stone sun
glares down on settlers in the remote forest:
a mythic country that disbelieves in itself,
but whose citizens yet declare allegiance,
and still feel mortal love and hurtful pain,
and drink to both from a bull's horn. . .

NEAR TOFINO, VANCOUVER ISLAND

The great auk and passenger pigeon
extinct a hundred years
close relatives of mine
at least compared to Tyrannosaurus
the lizard king whose tyrant head
was fringed with clown's tassels
his dinner-plate eyes
from an old horror movie
postmarked a hundred million years

Now the blue whale lollops
like a neighbouring planet
and orbiting the earth passes
my dirty Ford doubleparked
on the beach illegally
— the great blue whale
soon no doubt to die
five miles out at sea
spouts like a car wash

I stand for hours
to watch the great auks pass
Tyrannosaurus in his swamp
challenging eternal mud
glaciers receding at last
meltwater surging on the Ford

(Save me Save me maiden cries
in colour movies of the brain
I seize her by the hair and climb
high up some Quasimodo stairs
rest safe at last in Notre Dame)

My poor blood relatives
whose fossil bones are found
in limestone strata lying prone
or upright in earth catafalques
as if beseeching time more time
for reaching mammal status
or else descending back to slime
and praying to a lizard god

The man Neanderthal departs
and drives his car along the sand
(with seat belt buckled)
upright a little longer maybe
who loved a little
        thought a little
                and drank a lot
bequeathed the stars some Latin names
                    which they forgot —

THE NURSELOG*

These are my children
these are my grandchildren
they have green hair
their bones grow from my bones
when rain comes they drink the sky
I am their mother and grandmother
I am their past
their memory is my thousand years
of growing and waiting for them

Four hundred rings past
in my body count
there was fire
it touched me and I glowed
with blue fire from the sky
the sky was so close
it hissed and shimmered in me
then rain fell
Three hundred and fifty rings
past there was no rain
for many growing times
but when it came I heard
the forest talking together
How great a time ago
is lost but I remember
long-necked animals eating me
one great-jawed creature eating them
everything consumed everything else
and wondered if living was eating
Then the birds came
but strange birds like reptiles
with broad leathery wings
flapping and crashing through me
they changed to specks of blue
and orange and green and yellow
little suns sleeping in me

I remember this in a dream
when we all dreamed
as if I were an old repeated story
once told to me that I retell
And now the little green ones
nesting cleverly in a row
some love the shade and some the sun
another is growing crookedly
but she will straighten given time
one grows more slowly than the others
and has my own special affection
They are so different these small ones
their green hair shines
they lift their bodies high in light
they droop in rain and move in unison
toward some lost remembered place
we came from like a question
like a question and the answer
nobody remembers now
no one can remember. . .

*When a fallen log in the B.C. rain forest begins to decay,
its trunk becomes a nursery for hundreds of tiny tree seedlings,
all of them aligned in the same direction as the fallen tree.
Decay within the log raises temperature, hastening growth of
seedlings. Compressed annual rings in their heartwood record
the seedlings' growth before their roots reach soil; and then
they continue on toward the sky.

HAIL MARY IN DAWSON CITY

That fried egg on the horizon
hatched over Yukon mountains
is the sun
        I sit wedged
between Capt. Peacock and
his co-pilot on the flight deck
of a Fairchild aircraft
which is something
I never imagined doing
when I was a child prodigy
ambitious to be a sex pervert
as Gina the stewardess smiles
deciding we merit coffee
while the captain tells a story
about some Yukon alpiners
labouring up a snowy mountain
to find at the summit
(he pauses for effect)
— a pay telephone
Old Crow happens soon
we jigger along an ice runway
at the same village where Josie
says every morning on CBC
"Here are the news"
and it's 40 below zero
and I shoulda worn snuggies
Then the Richardson mountain chain
for a moment the yammering engines
silenced by a landscape so lovely
clichés are bottled for export
Nervous at Inuvik
because I can't see the airfield
on accounta the plane's proboscis
or hear the captain's story
about the Richardson Sasquatch
or the Mad Trapper of Toronto
because of Pratt & Whitney talking

All this only prelude to Dawson
and a doughnut-shaped hole in the overcast
we must penetrate to land
about the size of a manhole cover
with a sign stuck on a cloud
Admit One Fried Egg
— but no Fairchild airplanes today
For an instant I think
no more crummy poems
the world is spared that from me
but fail safe and I promise
a million Hail Marys or something
as we pass a mountain
with a raven perched there
so close to the wingtip
I ask if he's been talking
to Edgar Poe lately
We dive into clouds
and there is this moment
coming back to the world
with foolish conversation stopped
only a high singing sound
leaving the place of birds
and company of mountains
before continuing where we left off
before that blue interruption

ACROSS THE MARY RIVER...

Across the Mary River
there's a mountain made of iron
the oil rigs drill off Tuktoyaktuk
from artificial islands

At Aklavik and Inuvik
the breakup roars in spring
our fractured sky is upside down
with northern lights for witness

Flowers are fields and tapestries
five thousand miles across
they deafen eyes with whisperings
and blind the ears with loss

Seas are named for old dead men
explorers froze their blood
for kings remote on southern thrones
and queens pretending love

Dogrib and Slave are names of men
in lands of spruce and larch
their traplines cross grey parallels
their face the face of earth

The shamans of the Inuit
chant lunar prophecies
where giant dogs and snowmobiles
blaze weirdly in the sky

At Hay River on Great Slave Lake
masked welders work with steel
from Norman Wells their barges chug
to lands on the Beaufort Sea

The wide Mackenzie tracks ahead
past islands bathed in light
at Coronation Gulf grey wolves
run down the caribou

Across the Mary River
there's a mountain made of iron
and dwarfs of stone are spirit guides
of gods on Baffin Island

— they are mileposts of old passage
echoes of our hinterlands
plunging name-sounds
of things we felt or dreamed or imagined
this farthest earth
the shuffling roof of clouds
summers beyond our lives
with nothing of ourselves wasted
we used what there was
our bones flow onward
blood breaks and stops —

RED FOX ON HIGHWAY 500
         — near midnight

All I saw was the tail of him
the dream fox ahead of me
his rump a red light flashing
in a thousand movie still shots
(callipygous screenland special)
forty feet ahead of me
feet red hammers hammering
pounding away at the highway
light as air on the highway
running from death on the highway
he died or dreamed he did
— his tail a flat red poker
flung straight back toward me
his eyes overtaking his shadow
his tail bisecting the moonlight
he was fox fox fox

It was like a stage play
it was like my childhood nightmares
the guilt-ridden dreams of running
when all the adults chased me
but nobody ever caught me
it was like time had stopped for us
and never begins again
His shadow black as a monster
his shadow a soundless monster
stomping the dark ahead of us
suffering when we suffer
dying when we die

And I saw us running
I watched us doing it
the car the fox the shadow
those other selves for witness
— and I wondered about things

I wondered about all sorts of things
his face and what he looked like
apart from a million foxes
the rest of his breed and kin
and whether his foxy character
glowed in his brain and eye
and about this damn predicament
of having a dozen bodies
like fascinated observers
all of them watching us watching
deep in the moonlight forest
or under the bedclothes loving
or killing another animal
I was really philosophical
it was almost like a poem
and it had to end precisely
at ten minutes after midnight
so that I could drive to Belleville
keep an appointment in Belleville
and never forget a word

So here we are
and here we have been forever
running and running and running
your mate in the nearby forest
wondering where you got to
and failed to keep your appointment
an hour ago in the cedars
the mystery of why things happen
this way and never that way
the reason you kept her waiting
an hour or was it your lifetime
in case you go under the wheels

Of course I stopped
and gates of the moonlight opened
and lightly he stepped inside
— it was silent that kind of silence
when live events are waiting

jammed at the doors of time
what we meant to do in the moonlight
frozen in silver moonlight
then leaped into flux again
— he had to keep his appointment
no matter how late it was
and I had to drive to Belleville
both of us had our plans
plans of the utmost importance
for going on living longer
for eating and drinking and sleeping
and maybe loving someone
for killing other animals
for being noble and human
or fox fox fox

MAY 23, 1980

            I'd been driving all day
arrived home around 6 p.m.
got something to eat and slept an hour
then I went outside
and you know
— the whole world smells of lilacs
the whole damn world

I have grown old
making lists of things I wanted
to do and other lists
of words I wanted to say
and laughed because of the lists
and forgot most of them
— but there was a time
and there was this girl
this girl with violet eyes
and a lot of other people too
because it was some kind of a party
— but I couldn't think of a way
some immediate plan or method
to bathe in that violet glow
with a feeling of being there too
at the first morning of the world
So I jostled her elbow a little
spilled her drink all over
did it again a couple of times
and you know it worked
it got so she winced
every time she saw me coming
but I did get to talk to her
and she smiled reluctantly
a little cautious because
on the basis of observed behaviour
I might be mad

and then she smiled
— altho I've forgotten her name
it's on one of those lists

I have grown old
but these words remain
tell her for me
because it's very important
tell her for me
there will come one May night
of every year that she's alive
when the whole world smells of lilacs

IN THE SNOW

I wonder if that footfall
outside my door might be God
of course I know it won't be
but that kid I was wasn't
so sure as I am now
Sometimes in the snow
I followed tracks ending nowhere
and thought what do I care
whether some animal or some god
stopped in the snow thinking
I shall now perform my miracle
or have a shit?
Various curious noises
outside my door sometimes
unexplainable sounds:
on Mars tracks end in sand
on Venus something lopes softly
making ragged holes in the mist
each with a logical explanation
but hardly relevant
After all there's no good reason
for me to be standing in snow
up to my ass in a blizzard
wondering how I got there
or if there's something nose down
on the trail following me
some relentless something
there's no good reason at all
for it to laugh gloatingly

But various curious noises
outside the door right now
I do not care to investigate
such matters at all closely
prefer to retain my options
of belief or disbelief:
a god looking for shelter?
my own particular monster?
a beautiful glowing woman
searching for sexual succour?
— not what is most probable
the veritable terrestrial body
of Mrs. Alfred Eley

SPINNING
      for Colleen Thibaudeau

"Can't see out of my left eye
nothing much happens on the left anyway"
— you have to spin around right quickly
then just catch a glimpse
of coat tails leaving the room
(lace doilies on the settee)
light foot rising and disappearing
the last shot fired at Batoche
or maybe it was Duck Lake
— thought I saw someone I knew
and turned faster and faster
said wait for me
it was my grandmother I never knew
before I was born she died
— sometimes I turned fast enough
and nearly caught up with the sun
it bounded like a big red ball
forward and then went backwards
over the mountains somewhere
— thought I saw someone I knew
she was young in an old summer
I tried to remember very carefully
balanced on one foot
and concentrated and concentrated
lightfoot white feet in the long grass
running to meet her lover
I couldn't stop turning then
wait for me wait for me

INSIDE GUS

Ralph. His poems opposite. To him.
At least the form. Gnomic?
Simple beliefs? Tough beliefs
— tough to retain and nurture.
"Believe in nothing and poems." Not true.
"A gentle man," says Mark Pinchevsky.
Belief is gentle too. Sentimental?
Oh sometimes. If flowers and music are.
If love is. Love also is comic.
Is bone and blood. Is falling feather.
Useless? Well, subjective. Unstatistic.
Flowers and music. Chronicler of tag ends.
Notary of the unnoticed. Registrar of colour.
Wisdom? What's that? Who knows one?
Monk-scribble on sheep stomachs? Faith in blue
sky, goodness, clichés like banners:
our battered coffeepot brewing tea
in Sovietskaya Hotel, in Samarcand, Riga:
Betty in faded dressing gown fetching it:
he glances, absent, "Oh — thank you."

NIGHT SOFTBALL

Japanese Hitachi television is playing
American Phillips television at Ameliasburg
Frank Merriwell's and Babe Ruth's honest pitches
versus tricky oriental beanball curves
far east and far west twain meeting
in neutral Canada on behalf of commerce
The umpire is neither Hitachi nor Phillips
but a retired catcher with a bum knee
he works for General Electric in Belleville
and yells "Yer Out" at the Hitachi pitcher
who responds at full volume promptly
At the millpond this racket is reduced
and filters into the dreams of sleeping birds
it sounds like an owl killing mice
— the pond bullfrogs talk about summer
how tasty the insects are this evening
how handsome they are and females
— then a lurid obscene cussword floats
pondwards from the shortstop's mouth
(he'd booted an easy ground ball)
and all the bullfrogs nod together
intending to do just that in jigtime
they obey the injunction enjoyably
while the great yellow moon
hoisted by some celestial batsman
disappears beyond the village

NO SECOND SPRING
(Proposed atomic waste site at Mount Moriah in Hastings County)

1

Five thousand feet straight down
a shaft driven thru billion-year-old granite
equipped with electric elevators:
and there we shall hollow out great rooms
and place in those rooms the spent uranium fuel
contained in glass boxes
which shall again spend itself for 250,000 years
laying waste its powers of death
under the mile-high granite mountain
uranium "bundles" so hot the stone itself
would melt if not protected
shielded and guarded
under Mount Moriah

The noonday shadow of man
that lengthens and dies at evening
night-crawler on the face of time
— having given birth to a monster
turn in your sleep to see its face
this face outliving good and evil
magistrate above and below judgment
destroying all our categories
a black thing shaped like the human brain

The difficulty to be sure
is to be quite sure
whether that quarter-million years
of monster time travels forward
or that it possibly travels backward?
— or perhaps both ways at once
with a monster flip-flop
permeating time it becomes time itself?

2

We entered a turquoise continent
we hunters
following the mammoth with spears
falling rain painted the turquoise columns
and blue grottoes ran gleaming with rain
we were blue men we were turquoise men
we hunters
in light that filtered over our bodies
Our pursuer was a monster
a black man from the old time
with beast jaws and red gleaming eyes
then turning I saw that what followed us
was a man exactly like myself
but saw my own face reflected in rain
it grew black hair with great beast jaws
I turned then to pursue my pursuer
We stalked each other all that day
on the ice above Mount Moriah

3

"And it came to pass after these things
that God did tempt Abraham
and he said unto him Abraham
and he said Behold here I am
And he said Take now thy son
thine only son Isaac
whom thou lovest
and get thee into the land of Moriah
and offer him there for a burnt offering
upon one of the mountains
which I will tell thee of — "

And it came to pass
while a black face peered from granite
and soundless heat gushed in the stone

4

In the caves
that once were built by men
the children of men resembled their fathers
but were not men
These things have been told to me
by a different one
whose voice spoke in my head
and who still had something called sight
instead of this knowing we have
whether a thing is round or square
whether it is good to eat or not
friendly or unfriendly
or perhaps the thought of a thought
and which we know for only a short time
then lose the knowing
and cower in the rags of our caves
and hide till we know again
It is of small importance perhaps
but remains in my mind somewhat longer
for once it was told to me
that we are the children of men

5

Long Distance to the Ontario Hydro
Candu Reactor at Pickering

(Introductions, explanations, etc.)

Me — What does it look like? I mean
when you throw the stuff away?

Distant Voice — Black is the colour
of my true love's hair.

Me — Whaddaya mean by that?
Don't play games with me!

Voice — We don't throw the stuff away;
we store it carefully and safely
in underground caverns. It is very
hot stuff. Have you heard about
hot stuff?

Me (patient and resigned) —
I'm sure you'll tell me.

Voice — Black and liquid,
sometimes solid, containing
plutonium. So hot we call it
the China Syndrome.

Me — What's the China Syndrome?

Voice (dreamily) — The stuff is
so intensely hot it can melt
rock and sink all the way down
to the other side of earth and
reach China.

Me — I'm supposed to be the poet
here, not you.

Voice — I read your stuff.
You're a lousy poet, dad.

Me — Have you known how the blackness
covers your soul, and there is no light
anywhere; you cannot even imagine
light? When birds turn to cinders

in the sky, and beasts are carriers
of darkness? Have you known —

Voice — Shit!

Me — What?

Voice — Like I said: sometimes solid,
sometimes liquid, and hot as hell.
Loathsome and crawling like.

Me — That's all you have to say?

Voice — What would you suggest?

Me — Nothing more...

6

No second spring again
for you and I my love
our half life is thirty years
there is no second coming

We stood on Mount Moriah
counting from one to ten
and slowly we stopped our caring
or pretending we ever did

Say love when the ice gnaws deeper
say love when the fire eats down
could we waste a thought on each other
have we time for romance then?

Our myth is the cherished nonsense
that somewhere something survives
and the minds in our dying bodies
glow deep in a stranger's eyes

Sleep — would that have been better?
It is so — it becomes the same
when stars rush out at evening
my dust forgets your name

We were flesh but our hearts were shadows
we sent them off on their own
with all best wishes for happiness
sincerely yours goodbye

Reach out your hand my love

MANTIS

As for me: natural things would prevail
shadows would always move like sundials
their black rafters menacing and permanent
after a few centuries you could return
here and still notice ghostly 2" by 4"
landmarks of perpetual nothingness

As for her: in her wake permanence is flux
trees fall down shadows rearrange themselves
one thing joins itself to another
flowers whirling in mist are her compass points
and the bees have selected particular blossoms
which become vegetables at her direction

Unresistant I am manipulated
as an object placed or displaced
I cannot say no or yes only stand
thinking I have stood here a few moments
only where she has moved the shadows
into more symmetrical arrangements
and shortly no doubt will be dissatisfied
I shall be asked to stand thus and so
to enable the fulfilment of her purposes

I am sideways-on to the big events
mushroom clouds rise and are swept away
by high upper winds circling the world
and lying in bed enclosed by no light
I hear the plop and again plop of apples
falling outside from the over-ripe tree
and think to ask when she awakes
how she will dispose of those sounds
and hear my own small whisper not
of protest but some latent curiosity
in the disposable darkness
where I await my discoverer

THE DARKNESS

— particularly in Renfrew County
when I chased that porcupine
from cellar to woodshed
from lawn to road with flashlight
and felt affection for it
that I couldn't explain to myself
but do explain
as if it embodied all the lost
doomed animals crushed to death
on highways or swallowed and eaten
by fiercer animals — by man
Why should one comic beast
like a briar patch on four legs
be anything but that?
Anyway I'd stand there
beside the porch when bugs were gone
with everyone else asleep
looking up at that great ocean
that place where you're able to think
farther than you're able to see
billions of miles — or think you do
for surely observing light from that distance
is having your mind touch its source
having it brush against stars?
— my smallness therefore conversely important
my heart beating across that void
a tiny pump supremely unimportant?
Then I laugh
how ridiculous to invent methods
of deceiving yourself or pretending
you touched the far edge of the cosmos
Only settle yourself on the shore
of this bright sea this glittering enormity
and close your hand on a scrap of it
the darkness the massed nothingness
say I have grabbed some and held on

Surely if that frightened porcupine
could represent all dead animals
then I may allow myself this conceit:
to feel with hands and heart
the black reaches of light-absence
and the whip of comets
pulsing like swift little fish
when lights leap like car headlights
gleaming on wet pavement in the sky
What this comes to is religion
not the conventional stuff
but some lost kind of coherence
I've never found in people
or in myself for that matter
only in the unhurried natural world
where things are uncrowded by things
with distance between animals
star distance between neighbours
when the grouchy irritable universe
fumbles with understanding
and a god's coherence
                      Look down on me
spirit of everyplace
guardian beyond the edge of chaos
I may be a slight reminder
of a small tribe that occurred to you
when you were thinking of something else
even tho I am of little importance
and conversely of great importance
I am waiting here
until the dark velvet curtains
are drawn and the scrap of darkness
I clutched in one hand
has changed to light

FATHERS
    — for Ron Everson

This year I realized my dead father
was sixty when he died and I am sixty
but it's a year like any other year

(The annuals in our garden
are only two months old
just babies in the arms of earth
our perennial peonies are fifteen years
and fifteen years I've watched them rise
in scarlet jets from earth
— their time is earth-time and the sun's)

He was fifty-eight and suddenly
became an unexpected father
with a look on his face in old snapshots
as if he'd never enjoyed himself much
and two years later he was dead

In 1919 the year after the first war
there must have been several times
when the baby face and old serious one
looked at each other like blank coins
a thought registered a look stamped itself
something now forgotten was interchanged

It seems there should be more
something I can put my finger on
when a spark jumps between connections
a flame wavers from bone to bone
— reach out beyond the tangible
to those dark castaways
flesh of my flesh that dies
that touched and held

NORMA'S POEM

All my life I have been
my father's daughter
my mother's daughter
my sister's sister
my husband's wife

Now I am trying to find
the me who belongs to me

Only the sun and moon
are witnesses
only daylight and darkness
have taken my hand

My father the sun
my mother the moon
my sister the daylight
my husband the darkness
they have given me an old compass
they have taken me by the hand
I have entered into their safekeeping
I am becoming the earth

FOUND AMONG THE EFFECTS

As per your request
I will endeavour
to delay the aging process
against our meeting:
— keep my face calm
minus the usual joyous expression
to prevent crow's feet and wrinkles
refrain from lifting things
lest too much strain
be placed on arthritic knees
and deteriorating vertebrae
investigate the possibilities
of cosmetic surgery
within of course
financial limits
and failing that
read up on the methods
whereby Egyptian priests
endowed dead pharaohs
with a lifelike appearance
dogpaddling down
the River of the Dead
with lustful aspect
and fend off death
with one crooked finger
like a hopeless hitchhiker
up Styx Creek without a paddle
However I am beset
with dire forebodings
in the absence of Ponce
de Leon's fountain or
reasonable facsimile thereof

ignorant of recipes
devised by Huxley
to ensure his millionaire
survived the centuries
— and 6 foot 3 of me
grow suddenly ancient
at the sight of beauty
and die wondering
and die gladly

FOR BUMPER — who can't read

Growing older it's permissible
to be a bit intolerant
of people
but how can one be intolerant
of a dog with collapsed main sails
for ears and body a bluish pretzel
face a wet diaper
wriggling toward you on his belly
a hairy agnostic holy roller
approaching his god
It's as if your ancient wife
had a baby at age 60
reading up on late pregnancies
attending a class for old mothers
you staring at the little critter
bemused and helpless
brain softening with age
forgetting the names of aunts and cousins
and friends lost in your brain's mazes
trying to find their way back to civilization
Learn tolerance
of bed-wettings and midnight howling
frantic Buchenwald terror
at car travel
My scorn from watching the dog-people
parade their shitty pooches
across my mental lawns
no longer magisterial
It is senescence
decrepitude and dotage
a kind of laughter at yourself:

it is the schizoid heritage
from benches of old lost seas
when a mongrel emerges
from under cedar branches
you'd been sleeping on and decides
in that one instant whether to lick
your hand or bite it off

Lord Pooch
sired by Loudondale's Aristocrat
out of Misty Blue of Marbilland
gentry of Pooch's Peerage
blue blood of English manors
where your ancestors gambolled
while mine were stealing sheep
just north of the Scotch border
this dog salutes you

WHO KILLED D'ARCY McGEE?
(Ottawa, 1868)

Our hero the dead man
walked south from Parliament Hill
along Metcalfe Street
a full moon lighting the sky
gas lamps unlighted
(the city's contract called
for service only "during
dull periods of the moon")
then west on the wooden sidewalk
past horses' hitching posts
and Mrs. McKenna's Saloon
smoking a good cigar
puffing away at it
having spoken long and well
in the House and feeling empty
feeling empty of words
a tiredness in his bones
If anyone had been watching
(and someone must have been)
they would have observed his limp
because of an ulcerated leg
along the unpaved road
avoiding puddles and dirty snow
the new hat his wife had bought
for him in Montreal providing
a kind of jaunty look
Reaching 71 Sparks Street
and Mrs. Trotter's boarding house
he inserted his key in the lock
(everything completely ordinary
nothing disturbed the silence
the bald detective fast asleep)
then a rather odd sound:
noise like a car backfiring
but they weren't invented

The murder weapon was
a Smith & Wesson handgun
the bullet entered rearwards
penetrating the back of his neck
just right of the spinal column
tore out teeth and dental plate
emerged horizontally
and narrowly missed his upper lip

Any enemies the reporters
wanted to know later
of course many enemies
and one friend who wept
and helped carry the body

The killer may have been Whelan
or it may not have been
anyway they hanged him for it
he was a tailor

Leapfrog a hundred years:
Mrs. Trotter's boarding house is down
skyjacked planes fly round the world
nobody knows who kidnapped whom
— why just the other day Vermeer
was snatched from his museum wall
the kingdom of heaven is not at hand
it isn't even on the board at Lloyds
of London it's 10 to 1 on Armageddon
they've boobytrapped the Sistine Chapel
and bulletproofed the Pope in Rome
booked Count Dracula at the Gardens
with Buffalo Bill and Elvis Presley
— nothing has changed except the tempo

What point in all this grue and hag
I mean McGee
why mention things like this at all
so long ago it's meaningless?
The dead man rots in Montreal
and Whelan in a grave nearby
happy enough and so are we
The wife and friend are dead as well
(the friend of course was Whiskey John
Macdonald cold sober in Kingston)

In Ottawa old buildings lean
against the earth in afternoon
with the look of waiters tired of standing
and when we've all grown tired of it
we stay in bed a little longer
to read detective stories
Headlines shout
ballistics say:
MURDER WEAPON FOUND
WHELAN MAY BE INNOCENT
(and later in the back pages:
Investigators Baffled
Guns Unrifled in 1868)
— don't look at me
for I don't know
how can I tell who's innocent?
these are the facts
available for anyone
who wants to take the trouble
still — after more than a hundred years
why would anybody want to?
But that tailor now
a ready-made victim

it bothers me
his guilt or innocence
and nobody thinks of him
they remember only McGee
they think of important people
and that bothers me too
— who are those important people
whether alive or dead
about whom no one asks questions?
(In Montreal
at Côte des Neiges Cemetery
the bald detective lurking in forget-me-nots
slips handcuffs on a skeleton)

ANGUS UNLIMITED

He rode his motorcycle like a horse,
did Staff-Major Angus in World War 2,
and hauled his dog in a box behind:
in love with speed he took a turn too fast,
tumbled, broke his arm, flopped sideways
on earth, laid out like a chicken,
and the dog whined. In either ear
like bells rang silence.
For a jot of time Angus died,
blood rapids dammed, pulse stopped,
his face hunchbacked.
They picked him up they put him down,
they said absentmindedly sir,
and made off with his corpse
to the base hospital at Kingston.
Angus woke and cussed some. The dog barked
at nurse, orderlies and doctors.
The corpse said: I want my arm set just so,
then I can hold onto the handlebars. Proceed.
The doc demurred (he was a captain).
I'm Major Angus Angus thus replied
(in not quite those exact words),
I outrank you — and oh twas true,
twas true he did sans generals handy.
So here's what transpired directly:
motorcycle trundled inside hospital,
busted arm encased in plaster,
crooked enough to steer said cycle:
again dog sat in box behind master,
and all went merry as a bicycle bell.

Days months years decades
went by all of us at a slow gallop:
me an oft promoted then demoted
private man salute for wonder thirty
years hence and marvel at the little bastard's
gall panache and chutzpah chuckle
how he made things happen as if —
as if he knew I'd write this crummy poem
a century hence and ride his doggy motorcycle,
ride his Harley-Davidson into hell with him —
But hell I don't really want to go there,
and wouldn't if it wasn't for his beard,
and couldn't if I didn't see his silly face,
dead, and think: he loved things more than I did,
and therefore I'm unduly fond of him,
he's surrogate for me and others like me,
in fact for all the goddam murderous world.

Now on this calm blue and white
peaceful completely deceptive day,
consider rationally: could I possibly be wrong?
Perish the thought — how could I be deceived?
For that's exactly what the world is — murderous:
and if the ancient scraggly little man
who always refused to wear a hearing aid
had lived only a few moments longer
I would have convinced him this was so
by shouting in his ear:
but now because of all the earth
piled in between I can't do that.

COSMOS

There was such freedom
in our lovemaking
movements in stillness
islands of time

— the room had trees
and nesting birds
near far-off mountains
was a chest of drawers
— the bed grew meadows
where daisies bloomed
and brown-eyed susans
were flowering girls

Of course if we
never see each other
again there will remain
some small boy
continually surprised
by the tenderness
of other children
and the mountains
and the birds

SEASONS

Winter
in our thoughts of each other:
and I remember
the way another woman looked
at me as if I were the most
least thing on earth
and I was somehow I was
my own existence ended
and summer gradually coming on
to fill my vacuum in her mind
In late winter
before the melting time
the crocus stirred preparing
underground for its spring entrance
I lessened and grew more:
all least things affect me in season
all those remnants of memory
wind-worn and transparent
seen from the other side of now
as if I were looking at you
across some kind of curtain
and you were looking at me
as all things lessened
and grew more

Summer was very late that year
the birds seemed bewildered
questioning each other about snow
which some had never seen before
ice rimed the shorelines
and made small tinkling sounds
as if to say welcome
But wind blew colder
and they sent messages to relatives
farther south and said "Don't come
— they're waiting for us in the trees
and we never know which ones — "

It made no difference
the weasel's red eye glittered
foxes hunted and the human hunters
blew on their hands shivering
We shrugged close to the heater
and didn't speak
I would have said "Why do you hate me?"
but it was useless
we grunted with our eyes
Let me be quite forgotten
and come to think of it I want to be
a raindrop quivering slightly
off course of course falling
away from the sun maybe
finding the slim wingbones
of a bird among the cedars
a bird who may have thought
"oh dear — oh dear — oh dear"
before dying
let me be quite forgotten
as snow falls from the red sun
like a thousand thousand flowers
until our tracks are covered

GOODBYE

Be kind to her wind
work your mischief in hurricanes
towns and cities destroyed
and destroyed harvests
just beyond the horizon
be kind to her
in this iron world
where gentleness is rare

Be gentle sun
stay yourself
from unburned places of her mind
for she is unsure
that being what she is
is worth being at all
that she is not a shadow
called forth by accident
when the eager resilient
indomitable people
laughed indulgently
at those who were not
themselves
— be gentle sun

And moonlight I charge you
with your deceptive light
tell her for me
love does exist
sometimes invisibly tho
say it doesn't matter
that some people are strong
only a few a very few
are exactly what they are
and chime like bells

Be careful rain
soft rain of spring
track lightly in her hair
and touch her face
as if you were a lover
come with gifts
as if you knew
she might smile

And people
you who cross traffic lights
with confidence
you who negotiate
the curves of your agony
with patience and skill
and face dark paths
with fear perhaps
but face them
— think of her sometimes
in sun and wind and rain
and may all good fortune
attend your venturings

WRITER-IN-REZ

I am watching from my window
              students on campus
              some with beards
              books babies etc.
I count the ones without beards
                    girls that is
(there are twenty-seven)
hoping no males will knock on my door
                      — at this moment
a blonde in tight green slacks
strolls among the pigeons
and I am about to call
out that I have some crumbs
for the pigeons
            ask her
if she has crumbs for me
            KNOCK-KNOCK
Come in I say resignedly
a little guy does and shakes my hand hard
(why do little guys always do that?)
He wants a list of 46 books from me
for students to read over Christmas
dirty books that is
                but he says "salacious"
Migawd
       a Methodist minister
and the univ. prez will also
compile lists
            I can't believe it
All right then I will compile you
a list of 46 salacious books
he doesn't know what salacious is
shakes my hand hard and departs hence

                        By this time
the blonde is lamentably gone
replaced by a student with pimples
                        KNOCK-KNOCK
Okay okay — and it's this Jewish kid
he says he doesn't know
whether to be a great writer or worker
on a kibbutz in Israel
Why not do both?
It's the morality of it
                Huh?
If I'm a writer I'll be like evil Huysmanns
(I make a note to put Huysmanns on my list)
if I work on a kibbutz
I'll probably end as a saint
You got a problem I tell him
He fixes me with saintly evil eyes
and I tell him get the hell out
after we yak enjoyably an hour
By now the campus is quiet
blonde and pimples both gone
it's colder in here
the rad doesn't work
                KNOCK-KNOCK
It's this children's poet with dimples
her name is Molly
            I say Hello Molly
forbear telling her I hate smartass
kids who read poems and act superior about it
But it seems somebody sent back Molly's poems
they need work they said
of course she wants me to do the work
Awright awright
                let me read em
Of course they're shit
but now a problem

of morality does present itself
shall I say they're shit and advise
six months' labour in a kibbutz stable?
I give her my list finally
of 46 salacious books
extract the meat from *Fanny Hill* I say
the fat from *120 Days of Sodom*
send pemmican to publisher
and kick her ass out
                The blonde is back
                with pigeon crumbs
                I am thrilled
lean out the window flapping my arms
like a pigeon mentioning
I am in need of provender
but do not convince
nor is she distracted or even attentive
            KNOCK-KNOCK
I sigh wearily
            this goes on all day
            but Surprise
it's the blonde in green slacks
who is a pigeon fancier
her breast is heaving nicely
she wants an apology
I say Cluck Cluck
in lieu of same
look outside my window
debating a course of action
for a man of action
the moment is not propitious
no proper conjunction
of stars or pigeons or me
which is a pity
and her breast heaves nicely

THE STONE BIRD

Lady
     with the very modern illness
     agoraphobia
     but ancient as fear
     in a Greek marketplace
Lady
     I have seen your face
crumple and break in ecstasy
of terror of horror of being
alive in this sewer world
feeling alien thoughts beating
at your mind an office desk
protruding from one ear
a subway train from the other
bells clanging gongs shouting
while you're washing the dishes
or furtive
         among the bargain-seeking
                  hawk-eyed
shoppers in a downtown supermarket
                      Ah lady
you could not be one of them
the nickel-and-dimes people
the big-deal fast-profit people
nor the Great Artist with greater ego
intent-on-making-it people
         for lady you are people

     CLANG CLANG lady
goes some bell in your head
walking crowded streets sensing murder
beasts
     nosing your breasts
                animals
screeching at the doors of your body
         clamour of the mad
schizophrenes

                    BANG SCREAM HISS CRACK ROAR
— falling falling into that white place
without shadows
                        where the rivers are milk
            and Lethe dreams
and the landscape has no horizon

                        — and I do not say
that is not a good place to be
where the truly mad with wolf faces
cannot follow
                    but I do say
that given the seeds of murder
                    brutishness   madness
which are mingled and struggle together
inside that floating speck of life on the oceans
from which we emerged bewildered
                                    and wet
behind the ears
given that earth itself is a graveyard
built on dead bodies and decayed matter
of all those before us
                        animal and vegetable
a cenotaph and mausoleum of horror
— given that we are killers and rapists and lunatics
                                all these things
is Lethe better?
            tell me lady?

You have always had I think
                    some unidentified god
— of the corn harvest — of sun and moon
of simple order and arrangement
a god of reasonable things and gentleness
as an escape hatch of the spirit
                        I have one too
neither man woman nor neuter:

            once on an arctic island
at Kikastan in Cumberland Sound
in a moment of desolation
I laid my head flat against the island
a mountaintop of gneiss and granite
with ice floes silent nearby
and heard the heart of the world
                                      beating
        It was a singing sound
steady and with no discernible pauses
a song with only one note
like some stone bird with such a beautiful voice
any change of pitch would destroy it
                              Oh I know
a specialist of eye ear nose and throat
he would say it's a body sound
he would say blood capillaries indigestion
but the specialist would miss something
everything

        — that body-sound is earth sound
a singing sound of the past:
radioactive clouds condensing
rain beating the new planet
chemicals interacting on each other
to produce one-celled life
then dinosaurs then mammoths
                    and volcano rumblings
when tree ferns wove their nets in clouds
to cage the sky
when a bird was more snake than bird
its voice between a hiss and chirp
and the ice came
and there was no gentleness anywhere
but all that beginning earth
                    singing still

Lady
    those geologic ages
convulsions of history and pre-history
    all those dawn murders rapes and cruelties
        are condensed in one symphony
are singing in my ears
— a wind-song a sun-song
an earth song and a song of the sea
I hear it among the nickel-and-dimes people
I know it in the supermarket
I feel it waiting for that moment
of grace in the unexpected word
the pure spontaneous gesture
to join the swelling human tide
when all your weakness becomes strength
and your body floats in light

      Lady listen
the corn god and moon god
the god of warm summer days
as well as those dark blood-stained gods
plotting against life
      in their cities of the dead
— all of them are joined in our bodies
    Listen

— to sun-song wind-song and song
of the sweeping planets
their orbits unvarying
a quarter-inch after a million years
and the song of the corner grocer
an earth song I heard on an arctic island
the song of life
    Listen lady

Acknowledgements

Poems in this edition have appeared in: *Acanthus; Arts Manitoba; The Beaver; Brick; C.B.C. Anthology; Canadian Forum; Queen's Quarterly; Athanor; Black Moss Press; Aurora.*

The author wishes to express gratitude to the Canada Council and the Ontario Arts Council for assistance.